essenti♥als

the heart of the Christian faith

essentials

the heart of the Christian faith

LEE MCMUNN

10 Publishing
a division of 10ofthose.com

Unless otherwise stated, Scripture quotations are taken from THE HOLY BIBLE, NEW INTERNATIONAL VERSION (Anglicised Edition). Copyright © 1979, 1984, 2011 by Biblica (formerly International Bible Society). Used by permission of Hodder & Stoughton Publishers. All rights reserved. 'NIV' is a registered trademark of Biblica. UK trademark number 1448790.

British Library Cataloguing in Publication Data

A record for this book is available from the British Library

ISBN: 978-1-911272-00-7

Designed by ninefootone creative (ninefootone.co.uk)

Printed in the UK by CPI

10Publishing, a division of 10ofthose.com
Unit C Tomlinson Road, Leyland, PR25 2DY, England

Email: info@10ofthose.com

Website: www.10ofthose.com

essentials

CHAPTER ONE

reveal

PAGE 7

CHAPTER TWO

reject

PAGE 17

CHAPTER THREE

rescue

PAGE 27

CHAPTER FOUR

relationship

PAGE 37

CHAPTER FIVE

response

PAGE 47

questions

PAGE 51

CHAPTER ONE

reveal

Imagine you are on a train. You look up from your phone and notice a stranger has sat down opposite. How could you get to know them? I guess you could stare at them for a long time. It would be weird, but you could look at what they're wearing and what they're watching and who they're with and see if you can construct an idea of who they are. But at the end of the day it would all be guesswork. What we need is to engage them in conversation. We need them to reveal themselves. And when they speak we need to listen.

The same is true when a new neighbour moves onto your street. Or when a new student joins your course. Or when a new colleague starts working in your department. We can guess all we like. But if we want to find out the truth, we need to have a conversation. We need the person to reveal themselves. We need to hear their words about their identity.

The same is true with God. Most of us would like to believe there is more to life than we can see or touch. The idea of living in a pointless universe without a personal God who can provide us with purpose and protection is a frightening prospect to many. Whereas the possibility of belonging to and being loved by a caring God is absolutely thrilling. But how can we know the truth? How can we move from wishing it were true to knowing it is true? We need God to engage us in conversation. Everything would change if God turned up and spoke to us. We would be protected from self-delusion and guesswork.

Near the beginning of a short book called Luke's Gospel, there is a staggering claim made about the identity of a man called Jesus.

Listen to how he describes the moment when Jesus' mum discovers she is going to have a baby.

'...God sent the angel Gabriel to Nazareth, a town in Galilee, to a virgin pledged to be married to a man named Joseph, a descendant of David. The virgin's name was Mary. The angel went to her and said, "Greetings, you who are highly favoured! The

Lord is with you."

Mary was greatly troubled at his words and wondered what kind of greeting this might be. But the angel said to her, "Do not be afraid, Mary, you have found favour with God. You will conceive and give birth to a son, and you are to call him Jesus. He will be great and will be called the Son of the Most High. The Lord God will give him the throne of his father David, and he will reign over Jacob's descendants for ever; his kingdom will never end."

"How will this be," Mary asked the angel, 'since I am
a virgin?"

The angel answered, "The Holy Spirit will come on you, and the power of the Most High will overshadow you. So the holy one to be born will be called the Son of God.'"

✚ LUKE 1:26-35

Ever had one of those days? You wake up in the morning with a plan, but then something happens that changes everything, and your life is rerouted. Well, Mary was having one of those days. Minding her own business living out her days in a backwater town in the Roman Empire and then, bang. An angel appears and announces she will conceive, even though she will still be a virgin.

When we hear this we're not supposed to say, 'Well, of course, that's the way it was back then.' Angelic visitors were not the ancient equivalent of pregnancy test kits. Instead, we are supposed to ask, 'What kind of person is announced in such a dramatic way?' The answer is revolutionary! The claim is that Jesus was the Son of God in human flesh.

The word 'God' is a very elastic and elusive term. Lots of people like to talk about God, but not everyone means the same thing. For some God is a lonely individual. For others God is some sort of life-giving power, not personal, but present in some indescribable way, a bit like the force in *Star Wars*. But for Christians, God is much more like a loving community.

The Bible teaches that the God who is responsible for all the good and beautiful things, from the tiniest particle to the grandest planet, is a united family of three persons; the Father, the Son and the Holy Spirit. It's what Christians call the Trinity. It's the delightful conviction that for all eternity, at the very heart of the universe, has been a relationship of perfect love. And what we're told in Luke's Gospel is that Jesus is one of these divine three.

This revelation about God's identity is not supposed to confuse us, or send us to our calculators to work out how three can be one and one can be three. Instead, this news is supposed to thrill us!

It's no surprise that most of our songs are about love. That's what we long to experience and that's what we long to see. We may joke about needing a sick bag in the presence of a mushy couple. But genuine loving relationships are what make us smile. Love is beautiful to behold and creates joy in our hearts. So what a delight to hear that the God who made us exists as three eternal persons, who love each other perfectly.

It's fairly easy to work out why living in a world without a God would be depressing. Our lives would be completely insignificant. Here today, gone tomorrow and forgotten forever. But imagine living in a world where the God at the centre of the universe is a solitary individual. How disappointing this would be! He would know nothing of love for another. He may love himself but he would never have experienced that selfless and passionate giving of himself to someone else. But thankfully the Bible reveals that God is a united family of three persons; the Father, the Son and the Holy Spirit. And for all eternity each of the three has loved the others perfectly. What a thrilling truth! And what a helpful truth.

The existence of the Trinity explains why we love certain things. For example, why do we appreciate good friends and enjoy good company? Why is loneliness one of our greatest fears? The Bible says it's because the

God who made us is a relationship of three persons, and we have been created to live in a similar way. That's why relationships are so important to us.

Or consider how music works. Regardless of our musical taste, whether we like rock or classical or dance or heavy metal - why do we prefer the combination of distinct instruments playing together? Because the Father, the Son and the Holy Spirit have created a world that works like they do.

The amazing news of the Bible, or if I can put it like this, the stop-what-you-are-doing news of the Bible, is that 2000 years ago one of the members of this eternal family, the Son of God, took on human skin and bones in the womb of a Jewish girl called Mary. And then, nine months later, he was born into the world he created.

When a mother holds her child for the first time there is always nervous excitement. But can you imagine how Mary felt as she stared at this wriggling bundle of joy? Because she was looking down at the Son of God in human flesh.

The implications of this are huge! It means that God has engaged us in conversation. Therefore, we don't have to guess if there is a God and we don't have to imagine what he is like. Because when Jesus speaks he reveals divine truth. The only question is: will we listen to what he has to say?

CHAPTER TWO
reject

Emergency Departments are busy places, so unless there is a problem we keep our distance. However, just suppose I decided to visit when I was feeling in top physical condition. I wait my turn and when the doctor asks me what is wrong, I tell her that I feel great. Everything seems to be working as it should. My heart is ticking perfectly and my blood pressure is normal.

Since I'm there she decides to run a few tests anyway. She calls me in for my results a few weeks later. This time I'm less confident. I wait nervously until my name appears on the display beside the door. As soon as I sit down in her office I know something is wrong. With eyes full of compassion she tells me the news. 'I know you diagnosed yourself as healthy but the tests have revealed a growth. It's cancer. But don't worry, we've caught it early, and so we can treat you.'

At this point I have two choices. Either I can stand up in protest, ignore what the doctor has said and storm out of the surgery – angry that my day has been ruined, but confident my own verdict is true. Or I can remain seated, believe her diagnosis and entrust myself to the care of this knowledgeable physician.

Because Jesus is the Son of God he can accurately reveal our spiritual condition. Listen to what he says in Luke's Gospel.

'It is not the healthy who need a doctor, but those who are ill. I have not come to call the righteous, but sinners to repentance.'

LUKE 5:31-32

Jesus is making an obvious point. Only sick people need medical intervention. And he says the same is true spiritually. It's only sinners, that is those who have rejected God, who are in need of a saviour. Which of course begs the question: who are they?

It's popular to believe that most of us are in fine spiritual condition. At Heavenly Passport Control, most people are confident that they will get waved through as soon as the Border Guards hear about the decent life they have lived. But is this true?

Suppose we live in a country that is ruled by a generous king who provides everything his subjects need. Now one day every citizen decides to reject his loving rule. *En masse* we all decide to commit treason. Now, of course we don't call it this. Instead we talk about self-expression and personal freedom. But essentially what we do is reject the king who has the right to rule.

This rebellion doesn't look the same for everyone. Some actively slander the king. But most of us simply ignore him and get on with our lives. And on the whole, this doesn't lead to violent conflict between the people. The majority are still very pleasant. We nod at each other in the street. We say 'Good morning' as we pass by. But what fundamentally unites us is our rejection of the king, regardless of how we express it.

The reason God has the right to rule our lives is because he created us. We know from our everyday existence that those who make things, whether small or grand, have ownership rights over their creations. Whether that's a new business, a new song or a new book. If you create something, it's yours. You own it and therefore you have the right to decide how it should be used.

God has the right to command us because he is our Creator. We are his creatures. He made us. Therefore, he has the right to tell us how to live.

Our temptation is to think of God as a cosmic killjoy or a cruel master. But Jesus says this could not be further from the truth. God loves us. He cares for us. He provides for us. He gives us every good gift. And he wants us to thrive. In order for this to happen he gives us loving boundaries in which we are to flourish.

In fact, he acts like every loving parent does. No sensible father or mother allows their children to do whatever they like. That has disaster written all over it! If any of my three children approach me and ask if they can play lego in the middle of the dual carriageway at the end of our street, should I let them? Loving parents want their darlings to grow up and enjoy the world but in order for this to happen they must tell them what to do and what to avoid. Likewise, God gives us loving boundaries for our good.

We fear living under God's rule will make us miserable. But that's a lie! Passionate commitment to God and his way is for our happiness. Living with God in charge is not drudgery, it is delightful.

However, instead of listening to God, we all reject him. We all decide to live in his world, our way. Now we usually call this personal freedom or self-expression but its true name is cosmic treason or sin. Now the way I rebel may look differently from the way you rebel. But fundamentally we are all the same: sinners who love to receive God's gifts but who reject the Giver.

We hate thinking of ourselves like this, so we have a way of making us feel better. We compare ourselves to individuals who seem to be more sinful than us. We have our internal lists of people whose behaviour seems much worse than ours. And then when we need to feel better we reassure ourselves that even though we are not perfect, we are not like so-and-so over there. But that's a crazy way to live. It's like intensive care patients arguing about who is the sickest!

How serious is it to reject God? We complain about the cost of living, but what is the cost of sinning? Well, consider what we know from our experience of disobeying someone who has authority over us. In those situations what counts are not our personal preferences. No, what matters are the passions, priorities and prohibitions of the one in charge. And what happens when we disobey them? Some form of punishment follows our defiance. It's true in classrooms. It's true in companies and it's true in countries. Children get detention. Employees get sacked. Criminals get locked up. We know what is right.

Consequences follow disobedience. So how much more should we expect this to be the case with our Creator!

What are the consequences of rejecting God? Listen to what Jesus says in Luke's Gospel.

> 'I tell you, my friends, do not be afraid of those who kill the body and after that can do no more. But I will show you whom you should fear: fear him who, after your body has been killed, has authority to throw you into hell. Yes, I tell you, fear him.'

LUKE 12:4-5

Hell is the place where guilty sinners will suffer the punishment they deserve. And the punishment is to experience forever the full force of God's anger, which Jesus says should terrify us.

If we know someone is angry with us we normally try and avoid them. But we cannot avoid a future meeting with God. Everyone is heading for an unavoidable appointment with the perfect judge of the universe. And we don't have to speculate about the outcome. Our sentence has been revealed. We deserve to be punished in hell, because we have rejected God.

Is this fair? Does the sentence match the crime?

Well, consider how you would respond if you saw me in the park cutting a caterpillar in two. Suppose you then came back an hour later and saw me cutting a cat in two. That's more serious. What about if I was cutting a child in two? That's even more serious.

Do you see the logic? The consequences of an action get more severe if we harm a more significant creature. So why do we deserve hell? Well, because we have rebelled against our infinite Creator.

Many of us live in cultures which dislike hard truth. That is, we are repelled by information which makes us feel bad, even if it is factual.

This strikes me every time I watch *Strictly Come Dancing*. The celebrity may have completely forgotten the dance, dropped their partner and crashed into the band, but the judge who mentions any of this as a negative is likely to be booed! Living in such a sensitive culture means that any talk of hell will be even harder to hear. But Jesus loves us enough to tell us the truth about what is ahead so that we will appreciate and take advantage of the rescue he offers.

At this point we have an important choice to make. Either we can stand up in protest, disregard what Jesus says and remain confident that we are good people on the road to heaven. Or else we can believe the diagnosis of our heavenly physician and entrust ourselves to his care.

CHAPTER THREE

rescue

Learning another language can seem overwhelming. There are so many new words to memorise and so many ways to combine them. But here's my tip. In every language there is always one sentence you should learn as soon as possible, and it's this: "My friend will pay."

Rejecting God spells disaster for our eternal future. Cosmic treason is expensive. Because of how we've treated God, we deserve to spend eternity in hell. But here is the good news. Or more precisely, here is the stop-what-you-are-doing, wake-up-and-pay attention, eternity-changing, joyful news. Jesus came to rescue us from the punishment we deserve. He came to pay the price of our sin.

Sometimes we hear of individuals who deliberately put themselves in the way of danger to protect those they love. They are willing to pay with their life in order to keep their beloved safe. Elsa Delplace was such a person. She was 35 years old when she saved her son from certain death. They were both at a music concert in Paris on 13 November 2015, when armed gunmen burst in and opened fire on those inside. Instinctively, Elsa threw herself on top of her five-year-old son Louis. Wonderfully, he survived! But only because of his mum's sacrificial love. Only because she got hit instead of him.

Jesus did something even more amazing. He sacrificed himself to pay for our sin. Motivated by love, he chose to endure the punishment we deserve so we could be saved. He did this when his hands and feet were nailed to a wooden cross, and he was lifted up to suffer in our place.

Over the page we'll see how Luke's Gospel records the death of Jesus:

'The people stood watching, and the rulers even sneered at him. They said, "He saved others; let him save himself if he is God's Messiah, the Chosen One."

The soldiers also came up and mocked him. They offered him wine vinegar and said, "If you are the king of the Jews, save yourself."'

✚ LUKE 23:35-37

So why didn't he? He had calmed a storm, walked on water and raised the dead. So why didn't he save himself? Why did Jesus stay on the cross?

Imagine you are out in the countryside and you stumble across a group of school children who are in desperate trouble. They are in a fast flowing river, being swept quickly towards a dangerous waterfall.

Thankfully, you spot a life ring on the bank and throw it to the teacher. And then you watch as he swims across to the youngest child and places it over his shoulders. With great joy, you pull the child to safety. Then you throw the ring back and watch the teacher repeat the rescue. This happens again and again, but with each passing moment the remaining children get closer to the waterfall.

Eventually only one child is left in the water. But now there is no time to save both him and the teacher. So in one last act of dramatic heroism, the teacher puts the ring over the boy's head. And just as you pull him to safety, you see the teacher being swept over the edge.

Now if anyone ever asks you, why didn't he save himself? Because he was saving others!

He couldn't do both. It was either him or them.

The same is true with Jesus. He chose to stay on the cross in order to save us from the punishment we deserve.

Some people may wonder why God can't simply let us off. Why did Jesus have to pay for our sin?

Imagine you borrowed my smartphone. You are heading on a hike and want to keep in contact with your family. So I lend you my phone. You promise to use it carefully but on your trip you do the very opposite.

You throw it around, you drop it and you scrape it along a stone wall. When you return it, the phone is ruined. The screen is cracked. The back is scratched. And the sides are dented. Now you are very sorry for your behaviour, and I do want us to be friends. But who will bear the cost of your recklessness? It cannot just vanish into thin air. One of us will have to pay.

Likewise, our rejection of God results in a cost that cannot just disappear. Sin has a price and it must be paid. But here is the great news. Motivated by love, Jesus paid it for us. He bore the cost so we never have to. The punishment we deserve to experience in hell, Jesus experienced on the cross. He took the hit so we can be safe.

We know that Jesus died on a cross. But listen to how Luke's Gospel describes what happened after Jesus' body was put in a tomb.

'On the first day of the week, very early in the morning, the women took the spices they had prepared and went to the tomb. They found the stone rolled away from the tomb, but when they entered, they did not find the body of the Lord Jesus. While they were wondering about this, suddenly two men in clothes that gleamed like lightning stood beside them. In their fright the women bowed down with their faces to the ground, but the men said to them, "Why do you look for the living among the dead? He is not here; he has risen!"'

■ LUKE 24:1-6

This spectacular event in human history was God the Father's way of demonstrating that Jesus' suffering was enough. It is like a divine receipt, proof that Jesus' death on the cross was sufficient to cover all our sins.

Think what you need if a security guard stops you at the exit of a shop and accuses you of stealing. You are just about to walk outside and a firm voice says, 'Excuse me, can I look in your bag?' At this moment, what do you need? A receipt. You need the proof that the items in your bag have already been paid for. Well, that's what the resurrection does. It acts as a receipt. It assures us that Jesus' payment was enough to cover all our sins, past, present and future.

It's vital to know that the death of Jesus doesn't help us automatically.

Suppose a mob of people decide to trash Harrods, one of London's most luxurious stores. They spend hours causing millions of pounds of damage. Soon after they are caught they are confronted with the horror of their situation. They will need to pay for what they have done.

However, the vandals are told the amazing news that the owner is willing to pay the damages of anyone who is willing to join his company. He is planning to sell a priceless work of art to cover the costs. And he is promising a job with amazing perks: company car, personal shares and a generous pension.

Who benefits from this offer? Only those who commit themselves to the owner.

It's the same with Jesus. He has done everything necessary to rescue anyone from the punishment we deserve. But only those personally committed to him will benefit from his great sacrifice.

Many people find this whole idea of someone else paying for their sin very difficult. Think of the last time you went out for a meal with your friends. How did you settle the bill? Normally people pay for their own meals. It's a small example of a bigger principle. In life we take great pride on being able to pay for things ourselves.

However, if we decide to do this with our sin, we will spend eternity in hell.

But there is another way. If we embrace Jesus as our king we will experience an eternity of joy – all because our friend has paid.

relationship

Generosity is such an attractive quality. Think about how children respond when grandparents arrive with bags of presents. Or how we respond when a generous friend buys us the most expensive tickets for the biggest show in town.

God is generous. Look around you. Our universe is teeming with countless examples of his abundant kindness. And it doesn't stop with creation. God's beautiful extravagance extends to the salvation he offers.

Forgiveness alone would have been amazing. But the God who is Father, Son and Holy Spirit offers us much more. As well as forgiveness, we are invited to enjoy a relationship with each member of the Trinity.

Let's start with Jesus. How are we supposed to relate to him?

It's vital to realise that Jesus didn't come as a spiritual consultant but as a king. On the day of his birth, this is what an angel declared:

'Today in the town of David a Saviour has been born to you; he is the Messiah [that is, the promised King], the Lord.'

✚ LUKE 2:11

The difference between a king and a consultant is huge. Consultants never command. They will show us the options, but they never give orders. They will give us advice but they have no authority over us.

A king is different. A king is the one in charge. A king has the right to command.

Instinctively we don't like people telling us what to do. We may be happy to explore our spiritual options, but we would prefer to remain in charge of our future decisions.

But that's not what Jesus offers. He is the promised King, the one who deserves and demands to be in control of everything we say, do and think.

Now this isn't a bad thing. Jesus' rule is for our delight. Surrendering to this king will change us in beautiful ways.

Think of it like a house restoration project. You may have seen those TV programmes where someone buys a house that is a real mess. There are holes in the floor, leaks in the roof, and damp on the walls. But then, gradually, under new ownership each room is transformed until the end result takes your breath away. This is what happens to a Christian. Every part of us is gradually made more beautiful under the loving rule of King Jesus.

Obeying Jesus in a world where many people don't inevitably brings Christians into conflict with competing ideas. Therefore, anyone who follows Jesus should expect turbulence in their life.

There will be difficult situations with our friends, family and work colleagues. But being a Christian is worth it. With Jesus in charge, this life will be much more colourful, and the next life will be infinitely more pleasurable.

So that's how we are to relate to Jesus. What about the other members of the Trinity? When anyone follows Jesus as their king, they have the amazing privilege of relating to Jesus' Father as their Father. Listen to how Jesus responds when his followers ask him to teach them how to pray.

> "'When you pray, say:
>   'Father,
>   hallowed be your name,
>   your kingdom come.
>   Give us each day our daily bread.
>   Forgive us our sins,
>   for we also forgive everyone who sins
> against us.
>   And lead us not into temptation.'"

LUKE 11:1-4

No one is born as a child of God. We start off as his creatures. But when anyone commits themselves to Jesus, they are united to him and, as a result, they are given a place in the Father's family. We get to call *his* Father, *our* Father.

It's similar to what happens when people get married. Not only do they find themselves in a new relationship, they find themselves in a new family.

Some people were surprised when Prince William got engaged to Kate Middleton. She definitely wasn't poor but neither was she from royal stock. But when she got married at the spectacular ceremony that took place on 29 April 2011 at Westminster Abbey, she instantly became a member of the Royal Family.

When anyone becomes a Christian something even more glorious happens. The follower of Jesus instantly becomes a child in the Father's family. Their unity with Jesus is even closer than a marriage and it gives them a thrilling new identity. They are now one of the Father's children.

This truth has three wonderful implications.

First, it provides us with great security. Children who disobey their loving parents certainly damage their relationship until they are reconciled. The joyful intimacy disappears until the child says that very short but difficult word, sorry. However, their position as a child is never in doubt. Parental love is never removed.

The same is true for a Christian. The follower of Jesus is not perfect. We genuinely want to change and genuinely will change. But sadly we won't do everything God says all the time. But a Christian has nothing to fear. Unlike an employee who can be fired, a Christian is secure. Their position as a child is not in doubt. Neither past nor future sins remove us from our new family.

Second, it provides us with lots of brothers and sisters to love us, and many for us to love in return. Relationship with the Father is very personal, but it is never to be individualistic. Anyone who follows Jesus instantly has lots of siblings!

And, third, it provides us with a powerful motivation to change. We are now part of a new family. And so therefore we should seek to behave in the way revealed by our perfect Father. We are to learn and then embrace the beautiful passions, priorities and practices that we see in our new Father.

Now you may fear that you could never do this. Perhaps you've tried before and found it impossible to break the old habits. Well, listen to how Jesus' cousin describes him.

'The people were waiting expectantly and were all wondering in their hearts if John might possibly be the Messiah. John answered them all, "I baptise you with water. But one who is more powerful than I will come, the straps of whose sandals I am not worthy to untie. He will baptise you with the Holy Spirit and fire."'

■ LUKE 3:15-16

Jesus is the one who is more powerful. And the promise here is that he will baptise his followers with the Holy Spirit. The rest of the Bible reveals what this means. It is a pledge that Jesus will send the Holy Spirit to live within all those who follow him as king. And he will do this to help them change.

This means we don't have to be enslaved by our past or present circumstances. There is hope! Because of the presence of the Holy Spirit, power is available. Therefore, anger can be dealt with. Anxiety can be battled. Apathy can be replaced. Change is possible.

God is generous. We are offered a relationship with the Father, the Son and the Holy Spirit. The only question is: how will we respond?

CHAPTER FIVE

response

A Christian is not someone who simply believes in a God and is trying to lead a good life as they define it. No, a Christian is someone who trusts Jesus to rescue them from the punishment they deserve and is committed to him as their king. As a result, they have benefitted from Jesus' great sacrifice on the cross. They will never experience the punishment they deserve; they are now one of the Father's children; and they enjoy the presence of the Holy Spirit in their life.

We don't need to know everything about Jesus before we decide to follow him. It's like getting married. People don't know everything about each other before they make their promises. No, they get to the point where they know enough about the other person to say, 'This person is for me.' It's the same with Jesus.

If you have believed what you have read in this book then you are ready to become a Christian. One of the ways you can do this is by saying the following prayer.

Jesus, I am amazed by your love for me. Thank you for sacrificing yourself so I can be rescued from the punishment I deserve. From this point onwards, I want to trust you as my saviour and obey you as my king.

Father, I am sorry that I've rebelled against you. But thank you for embracing me as your child. Please help me, by the power of the Holy Spirit, to change so that I become more like you.

Amen.

If you have genuinely committed yourself to Jesus using these words then be encouraged. You are now a child in the Father's family. And the powerful Holy Spirit dwells within you. What great news! Your next step is to get involved in a local Bible teaching church.

You may not be ready to follow Jesus at this point. You may still have questions that need answering. In this case, we'd still love to help you find out more. We have many other resources to help. Do email us and we can suggest what you would find useful: *info@lifeessentials.org.uk*

You may also like to check out our website: *www.lifeessentials.org.uk*

questions

The following pages contain questions to help you clarify what you have read. You may find it useful to talk about them with a friend, family member or work colleague.

These questions can also be used to help discuss the Essentials videos. These short films explore the heart of the Christian faith and can be accessed for free on our website: *www.lifeessentials.org.uk*

questions from reveal

'...God sent the angel Gabriel to Nazareth, a town in Galilee, to a virgin pledged to be married to a man named Joseph, a descendant of David. The virgin's name was Mary. The angel went to her and said, "Greetings, you who are highly favoured! The Lord is with you."

Mary was greatly troubled at his words and wondered what kind of greeting this might be. But the angel said to her, "Do not be afraid, Mary, you have found favour with God. You will conceive and give birth to a son, and you are to call him Jesus. He will be great and will be called the Son of the Most High. The Lord God will give him the throne of his father David, and he will reign over Jacob's descendants for ever; his kingdom will never end."

"How will this be," Mary asked the angel, "since I am a virgin?"

The angel answered, "The Holy Spirit will come on you, and the power of the Most High will overshadow you. So the holy one to be born will be called the Son of God."'

✚ LUKE 1:26-35

1. What kind of God would you like to exist? How persuaded are you that God is real?

2. Luke's Gospel claims that Jesus is the Son of God. How does this compare with your view of Jesus?

3. Jesus says God is a loving community of three divine persons, the Father, the Son and the Holy Spirit. Does this make sense? Do you think this is good news?

4. How should we respond to the news that one of the Divine Three has engaged us in conversation?

questions from reject

'It is not the healthy who need a doctor, but those who are ill. I have not come to call the righteous, but sinners to repentance.'

⊞ LUKE 5:31-32

'I tell you, my friends, do not be afraid of those who kill the body and after that can do no more. But I will show you whom you should fear: fear him who, after your body has been killed, has authority to throw you into hell. Yes, I tell you, fear him.'

⊞ LUKE 12:4-5

1. Why might God have the right to tell us how to live?
2. How convinced are you that you are a sinner?
3. Do you think the punishment Jesus describes fits the crime?
4. How do you think you will respond to Jesus' diagnosis of our spiritual health?

questions from rescue

'The people stood watching, and the rulers even sneered at him. They said, "He saved others; let him save himself if he is God's Messiah, the Chosen One."

The soldiers also came up and mocked him. They offered him wine vinegar and said, "If you are the king of the Jews, save yourself."'

▣ LUKE 23:35-37

'On the first day of the week, very early in the morning, the women took the spices they had prepared and went to the tomb. They found the stone rolled away from the tomb, but when they entered, they did not find the body of the Lord Jesus. While they were wondering about this, suddenly two men in clothes that gleamed like lightning stood beside them. In their fright the women bowed down with their faces to the ground, but the men said to them, "Why do you look for the living among the dead? He is not here; he has risen!"'

▣ LUKE 24:1-6

1. Can you see why Christians celebrate the death of Jesus?
2. Why do Christians think the resurrection of Jesus is such good news? How convinced are you that it happened?
3. How do you feel about someone else paying for your sin?
4. Where do you think you'll be in 2000 years?

questions from relationship

'Today in the town of David a Saviour has been born to you; he is the Messiah [that is, the promised King], the Lord.'

✚ LUKE 2:11

'''When you pray, say:
  'Father,
  hallowed be your name,
  your kingdom come.
  Give us each day our daily bread.
  Forgive us our sins,
  for we also forgive everyone who sins against us.
  And lead us not into temptation.'''

✚ LUKE 11:1-4

'The people were waiting expectantly and were all wondering in their hearts if John might possibly be the Messiah. John answered them all, "I baptise you with water. But one who is more powerful than I will come, the straps of whose sandals I am not worthy to untie. He will baptise you with the Holy Spirit and fire.'"

▣ LUKE 3:15-16

1. Do you think God is generous?
2. How do you feel about people telling you what to do? What motivations are there to obey Jesus as king?
3. Why do Christians think it is such good news to be one of the Father's children?
4. What areas of your life would you like to see transformed?

10 Publishing

10Publishing is committed to publishing quality Christian resources that are biblical, accessible and point people to Jesus.

www.10ofthose.com is our online retail partner selling thousands of quality books at discounted prices.

For information contact: **info@10ofthose.com** or check out our website: **www.10ofthose.com**